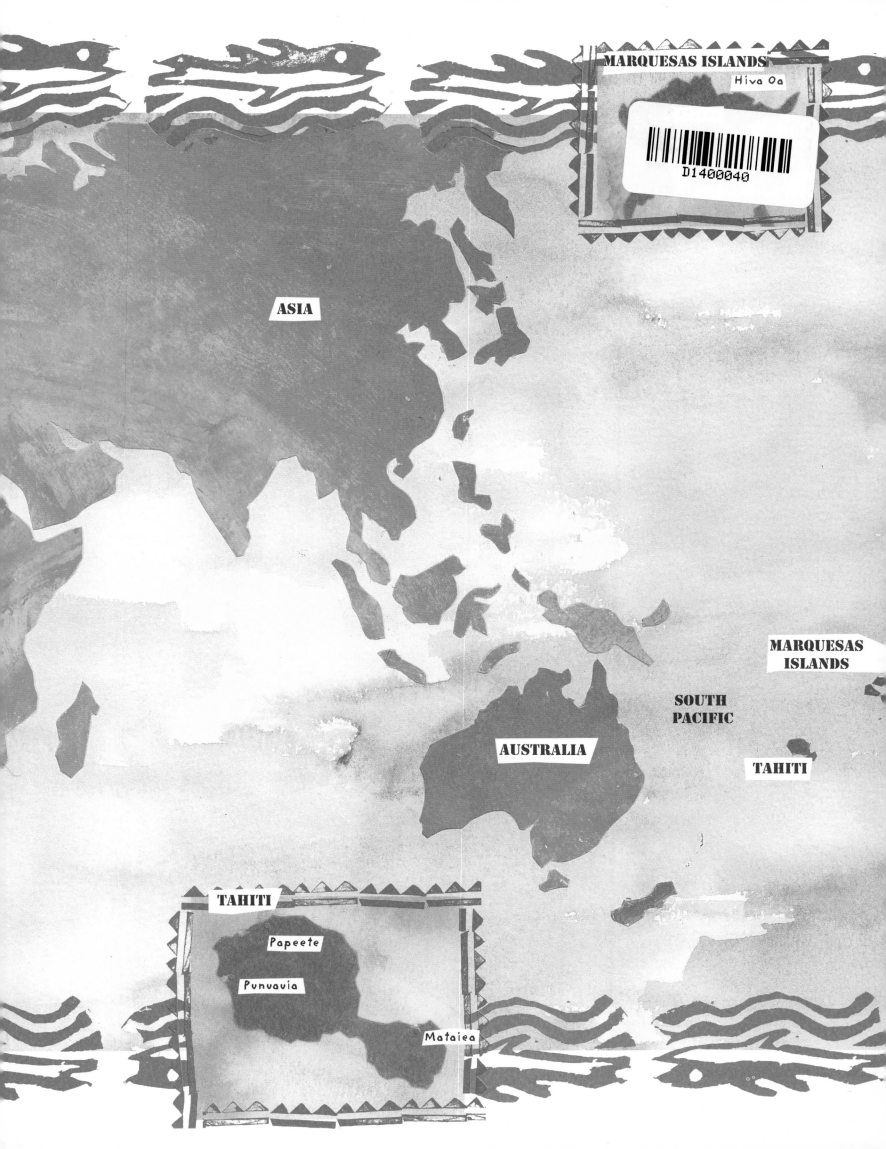

MARQUESAS ISLANDS

Hiva Oa

ASIA

MARQUESAS
ISLANDS

SOUTH
PACIFIC

AUSTRALIA

TAHITI

TAHITI

Papeete

Punuavia

Mataiea

Ceciel de Bie & Martijn Leenen

Paul Gauguin

See and do children's book

**The artists' guesthouse
of Madame Gloanec
in Pont-Aven**

**The harbour of Pont-Aven
in Brittany**

The yellow House at Arles

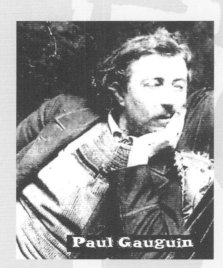

We would like to thank Sjraar van Heugten for his advice, and everyone else who was involved in the making of this book.

Paul Gauguin

'Where can I find the paradise of my dreams?' wondered Paul Gauguin, a French artist who lived from 7 June 1848 to 8 May 1903. 'It must be somewhere… I would really be able to paint there, and finally I'd be happy.' It made no difference to Paul that he would have to travel all the way to the other side of the world to find his paradise.

In this book you can read all about Paul's search for paradise, and his paintings. You can get busy yourself too, with drawing and painting projects. Would you like to join Paul Gauguin on his journey?

**Arrival by steamboat
in Tahiti**

**Tahitian landscape with
mountains and palm trees**

Tahitian fishermen

1889

1889

1890

The Eiffel Tower in Paris

The pavilion of the French colonies at the World Fair

The harbour of Le Pouldu in Brittany

What's in this book?

Get busy!

A rainy day in lively Paris

Tahitian boy on horseback, adorned with flowers

Tioke in Atuona on the Marquesas Islands

1894

1895

1902

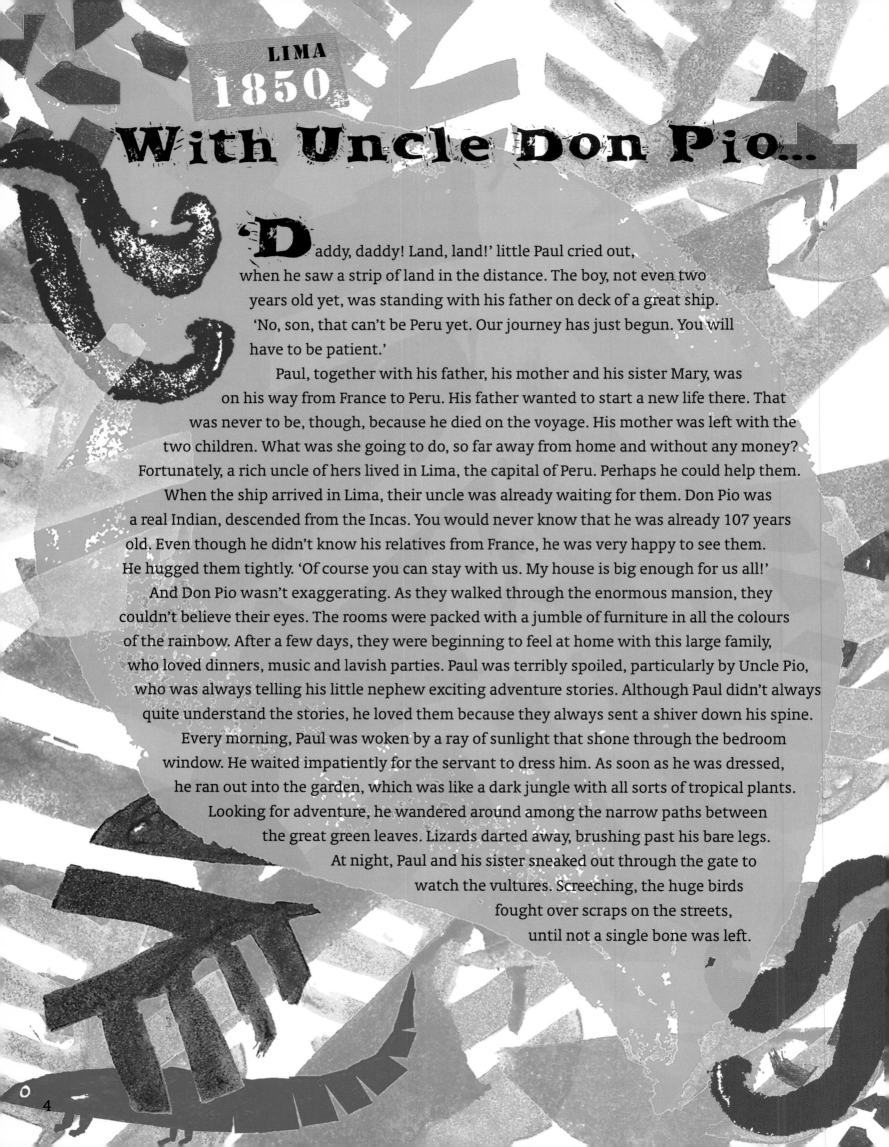

With Uncle Don Pio...

'Daddy, daddy! Land, land!' little Paul cried out, when he saw a strip of land in the distance. The boy, not even two years old yet, was standing with his father on deck of a great ship. 'No, son, that can't be Peru yet. Our journey has just begun. You will have to be patient.'

Paul, together with his father, his mother and his sister Mary, was on his way from France to Peru. His father wanted to start a new life there. That was never to be, though, because he died on the voyage. His mother was left with the two children. What was she going to do, so far away from home and without any money? Fortunately, a rich uncle of hers lived in Lima, the capital of Peru. Perhaps he could help them. When the ship arrived in Lima, their uncle was already waiting for them. Don Pio was a real Indian, descended from the Incas. You would never know that he was already 107 years old. Even though he didn't know his relatives from France, he was very happy to see them. He hugged them tightly. 'Of course you can stay with us. My house is big enough for us all!'

And Don Pio wasn't exaggerating. As they walked through the enormous mansion, they couldn't believe their eyes. The rooms were packed with a jumble of furniture in all the colours of the rainbow. After a few days, they were beginning to feel at home with this large family, who loved dinners, music and lavish parties. Paul was terribly spoiled, particularly by Uncle Pio, who was always telling his little nephew exciting adventure stories. Although Paul didn't always quite understand the stories, he loved them because they always sent a shiver down his spine. Every morning, Paul was woken by a ray of sunlight that shone through the bedroom window. He waited impatiently for the servant to dress him. As soon as he was dressed, he ran out into the garden, which was like a dark jungle with all sorts of tropical plants. Looking for adventure, he wandered around among the narrow paths between the great green leaves. Lizards darted away, brushing past his bare legs. At night, Paul and his sister sneaked out through the gate to watch the vultures. Screeching, the huge birds fought over scraps on the streets, until not a single bone was left.

and with Uncle Zizi

When Paul was seven years old, the bags were packed again and they returned to France. Paul's mother was homesick. Uncle Zizi from Orleans had invited her and her children to come and stay with him.

Uncle Zizi lived alone in a big, imposing house. Every morning, he went to the office. In the evenings, he worked in the garden. The plants and flowers were all lined up neatly in rows. There wasn't a single weed to be seen.

The calm, kind man was glad of the activity in his quiet house. But for Paul it was no fun at all. One day, when it was raining again and he wasn't allowed to go outside, he asked his uncle, 'Uncle Zizi, will you tell me a story?' His uncle meant well, but the stories he told weren't exciting at all. Paul didn't like to play with his sister either. Most of the time they would end up fighting, because Mary always tried to boss him around.

One sunny morning Paul was absent-mindedly gazing at a picture of a traveller walking through a sunny landscape, whistling merrily as he went. His luggage was tied up in a cloth, which was dangling from a stick he carried over his shoulder. 'I'm going to travel too,' Paul thought to himself. He had had enough of living with Uncle Zizi. He filled his handkerchief with sand and tied it to a branch he had found on the street. He set off on his journey in high spirits. Paul had already gone a long way when it began to get dark. The butcher, who was just delivering his last order of the day, bumped into him on the street. 'What are you doing so far away from home?' he asked, surprised. 'Does your mother know that you're wandering around here all by yourself? Come on, I'll take you home.'

Let's leap forward in time. It is 1888 – Paul is now forty years old. He has gone to Brittany to paint. Do you want to go and see what Paul Gauguin is doing there?

The Vision after the Sermon, 1888

Breton Girls Dancing, 1888.

PONT-AVEN
1888

Madame Gloanec was getting ready for the new summer season. She was busy cleaning the windows of her guesthouse when Paul arrived. 'You're early this year, Monsieur Gauguin; the other painters aren't here yet. Your room is ready, though.' Paul would be staying in the guesthouse again for the next few months. It was cheap and cheerful there. He wasn't the only one who thought so. In the summer it was fully booked up by artists, who also wanted to escape from noisy Paris. Paul was glad to have the place all to himself for a while. After the hustle and bustle of the city he needed some time to unwind and settle down – even here in Pont-Aven, which he knew like the back of his hand.

After he had unpacked, Paul wandered through the streets. He breathed a sigh of relief. He was glad to see that nothing had changed in the beautiful village – it was as if time had stood still. People were standing in groups in the village square. The sunlight glinted off the white caps of the Breton women. They talked about the weather, the harvest and fishing.

'I'd rather be a painter than a businessman'

'I wish Mette and the children were here,' thought Paul. 'Then I could show them the beautiful Breton landscape. How long has it been since I last saw them?'

Paul and his Danish wife Mette had lived in Paris for ten years. Paul worked as a trader on the stock exchange, and he earned enough money to live in luxury. Every Sunday, Paul went out to paint in the countryside. On his way home he often dropped in on his friend Gustave Arosa.

When Gustave opened the door one day, he said, 'Paul, come in quickly. I've just bought a beautiful painting by Monet. It's an impressionist landscape. Tell me what you think of it.' Paul carefully examined the painting. 'I say, Gustave! This has been painted so freely. You can see every brushstroke. And the colours – they're so bright! This is completely different from the landscape I painted today. I'm going to try painting this way too!'

Paul usually meant to visit his friend for just a short while, but he always ended up staying longer. Gustave was a real art lover. When he started talking about his collection of paintings, there was no stopping him. The more Paul learnt about painting, the more keen he became.

After a crisis on the stock exchange in 1882, Paul's earnings began to fall. 'This is the perfect time to stop doing this work,' he told Mette one day. 'I'm going to be a painter.' His wife was shocked. 'But what about me and the children?' she asked. Paul tried to reassure her. He was so sure that he could earn enough money from his painting, that she believed him. After a while, though, Paul and Mette found out that no one wanted to buy his paintings. They even had to move to another town, because Paris was too expensive. Within a year they had spent almost all of their savings. This was too much for Mette. She left with their five children, and went to stay with her family in Denmark. Paul stayed behind, alone, in France.

Experimenting with colours and shapes

'What a discovery!' Paul mumbled, while he was at work in his studio. 'The way I can paint the landscape using big shapes and flowing lines – I wouldn't have dared to do it like that just a few years ago.' In Brittany, Paul had discovered a whole new way of painting. A painting would begin to take shape in his mind during his long walks through the Breton hills. Paul looked around him carefully, and tried to remember all he saw. Only when he returned to his studio did he begin to paint the rolling hills, the turbulent sea, the rocky coasts and the people he had seen on his walks. The paintings no longer had to look just the same as what he'd seen, and the colours could be different to the ones you find in nature. Working this way, he never knew in advance what a painting was going to look like, and every landscape he painted was a surprise. One day, in a fit of fiery passion, he even painted the grass in one of his pictures red!

9

Look on pages 6-7

Do you see the river Jacob has
to cross in the painting?

What colours
did Paul use
for the painting?

Can you see the faces
of the women?

Can you see the
blades of grass?

'The Vision after the Sermon'

Paul loved to chat with the people of the village. That's how he learned that the Breton women were very religious. Sometimes their stories inspired him to paint.

One day, the priest had been reading from the Bible during morning Mass. One of the women told Paul the story as if she'd been there herself. 'Jacob was travelling back to his homeland, together with his two wives, eleven children and their servants. It was a long and exhausting journey. One night, they had to cross a river. Jacob waited until everyone was safely on the other side. But before he could cross the river himself, he suddenly found himself in a fight with a stranger. The two men struggled until the following morning. Then the stranger surrendered. He turned out to be an angel. Jacob had defeated an angel! Isn't that a miracle, Monsieur Gauguin?'

In his imagination, Paul could see the women coming out of church and watching the angel and Jacob fighting on the grass. They stood back in a circle and hardly dared to look. That was how he got the idea for this painting.

Paul wanted to give the painting to the old church of Nizon. He thought it belonged there. On the back he wrote, 'This is a gift from Tristan Moscoso.' That was the Peruvian name he had made up for himself. With a group of friends, he carried the canvas through the fields to the village, which was near Pont-Aven. They found a good spot and hung it on the wall. But the priest refused the gift. He was afraid that people wouldn't want such a strange painting in their church. That's why it was quickly removed.

The guesthouse dining room

During the daytime, Paul worked alone. In the evenings, he usually dined in the guesthouse, where he would meet the other artists. One warm evening in August, there were two new guests at the long dining table. The young painter Emile Bernard and his sister Madeleine introduced themselves to Paul. 'Would you please take a look at my drawings of Brittany, Monsieur Gauguin?' Emile asked during dinner. He pushed a large pile of drawings across the wooden table

Still Life with Three Puppies, 1888. Madame Gloanec's dog has had puppies. They're drinking milk from a bowl on the table. Paul wasn't sitting at the table when he painted the puppies. Where was he? If you look at the painting, it's as if you're flying towards it and coming in to land on the table. Paul has rounded off the shapes and painted dark lines around them. Everything is so simple you can hardly see any details. Look at the puppies' noses, for instance.

towards Paul. Paul slowly thumbed through the pile. 'This youngster has talent,' he thought to himself, 'I could have drawn these myself.' He slapped Emile heartily on the back. 'You're exploring the same ideas as I am. You draw the landscapes with big, simple shapes and flowing lines. We could learn a lot from each other.' From that moment on, Emile and Paul often worked together.

A letter from the painter Vincent van Gogh

'I've just received a letter from Vincent,' Paul told Emile one evening. 'He sends you his regards. He really loves the sunny south. The things he has written about his latest paintings make me very curious. Vincent wants to start a house for artists in Arles. He's rented a house with four rooms, where artists can come to stay and work. I'm the first one he's invited. In every letter he asks me when I'm coming. I'm not sure if that's such a good idea, though – the two of us are so different!'

11

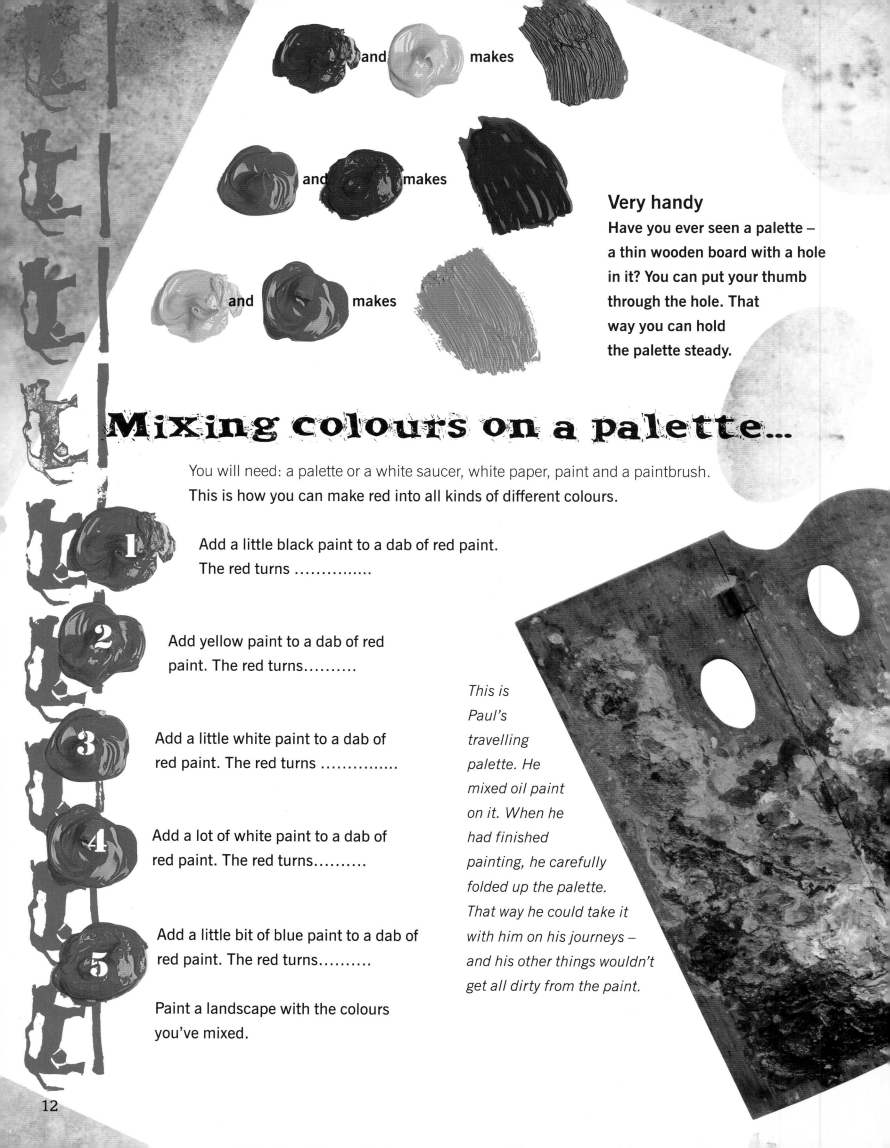

and   makes

and   makes

and   makes

Very handy

Have you ever seen a palette –
a thin wooden board with a hole
in it? You can put your thumb
through the hole. That
way you can hold
the palette steady.

Mixing colours on a palette...

You will need: a palette or a white saucer, white paper, paint and a paintbrush.
This is how you can make red into all kinds of different colours.

1 Add a little black paint to a dab of red paint.
The red turns ....

2 Add yellow paint to a dab of red
paint. The red turns..........

3 Add a little white paint to a dab of
red paint. The red turns ....

4 Add a lot of white paint to a dab of
red paint. The red turns..........

5 Add a little bit of blue paint to a dab of
red paint. The red turns..........

Paint a landscape with the colours
you've mixed.

*This is
Paul's
travelling
palette. He
mixed oil paint
on it. When he
had finished
painting, he carefully
folded up the palette.
That way he could take it
with him on his journeys –
and his other things wouldn't
get all dirty from the paint.*

Get busy!

Ravine of the Creuse is an impressionist landscape painted in 1889 by Claude Monet (1840-1926). The impressionists painted outdoors, using bright colours and loose brushstrokes. They applied their paint directly from the tube, without mixing it on a palette. 'You can only paint an impression of a landscape,' they said. 'The light keeps changing all the time, so that the landscape looks different every minute.' In the details of Monet's painting you can see free, colourful strokes of paint. You can't immediately tell what it is. When you look at the painting from a distance, the colours blend… and suddenly you see a landscape. Can you find the five details in the painting?

These are five details from Monet's painting. This is what you see when you take a closer look.

and mixing colours on the painting

You will need: paper, paint and paintbrushes.

Paint your own impressionist landscape. Use the paint directly from your paint box or tube. Paint with small strokes or dots, just like Claude Monet.

Harmonising colours

The colours above that are next to each other harmonise perfectly with each other. So green goes well with yellow, and yellow goes well with orange.

…and complemental colours

The three colour combinations below contrast sharply. If you use these colours next to each other they will shimmer slightly before your eyes.

Café at Arles, 1888

This is the self-portrait that Paul sent to Vincent van Gogh in 1888. He has painted a portrait of Emile Bernard in the background.

In Arles, Paul painted a portrait of Vincent van Gogh painting sunflowers.

ARLES
1888

In late October, facing the prospect of a cold winter, Paul decided to go to Arles after all. He arrived in town at the crack of dawn. It was very quiet; everyone was still fast asleep. He drank a cup of coffee in a small all-night café, and waited for it to get light. The barman looked over at him and said, 'You're Vincent van Gogh's friend, aren't you? I recognise you from a portrait I saw at his house.' He showed Paul the way to the yellow house at Place Lamartine.

Vincent seemed to have been awake for a long time. Proudly he showed his guest around. He had furnished Paul's room with the most beautiful furniture and objects he could find. In his own bedroom there were only very ordinary things. He had even painted two pictures of sunflowers, especially for Paul's room. 'These are the most beautiful paintings you've ever made,' Paul said, amazed. 'I'm curious to see what else you've done.'

That afternoon, Vincent couldn't wait any longer. He was bursting with impatience to show Paul the landscape he had grown to love so much. As they went for a long walk, Paul fell rather quiet. This was not at all what Vincent's stories had led him to believe. He hadn't expected these dry, barren plains. But he didn't want to upset his friend, so he didn't say anything.

An attractive offer

Once Paul wrote to his wife Mette: 'People love my work. What good is that, though, if no one wants to buy my paintings and I often haven't got anything to eat for three days.' For the time being, Paul didn't have to worry about money.

Theo, Vincent's younger brother who lived in Paris and was an art dealer, had made him an attractive offer. In exchange for one painting a month, he would give Paul a small amount of money. Theo would then try to sell these paintings in his art gallery.

Paul and Vincent tried to live as cheaply as possible. That's why they didn't eat at the café every night. It was just as well that Paul liked to cook! One day, Vincent insisted on making some soup. How he could make something so simple taste so awful was a mystery to them both. They couldn't stop laughing about it. 'You'd better stick to mixing paint instead of ingredients for soup,' Paul said, 'that would be much healthier for both of us!'

Just too different

'Oh, it's nice to see my own painting again,' said Paul when he saw his self-portrait hanging on the wall. Vincent had asked Paul and Emile to paint portraits of each other. Instead, they had both painted self-portraits, which they had sent to their friend.

'I was so glad to see your faces again that I hung these portraits on the wall straight away,' said Vincent. 'It also gave me a chance to compare our ways of painting. I use thick paint, and my brushstrokes are plain to see. You use such a thin layer of paint that the threads of the canvas show through, and your brushstrokes are much more delicate than mine.'

'That's not the only difference,' said Paul. 'I work from memory. First I study the landscape carefully. I walk through it and make sketches on paper. It's only when I'm back in my studio that I start painting. The landscape I paint doesn't have to be exactly the same as what I saw outside. That just makes my paintings more exciting: I never know in advance what they will look like. You should try it too.'

'Why not?' thought Vincent, who admired Paul as a painter. He started on a new painting straight away. But he soon realised that painting from memory just wasn't for him. He preferred to go out with his paints and his easel, so that when he saw something that caught his eye, he could get down to work straight away.

There was one thing that Paul and Vincent did have in common though: all they could think about was painting, painting, painting! They would work deep into the night. But their ideas about painting were very different. Paul didn't like Vincent's favourite painters, and Vincent didn't like Paul's. Their long discussions began to get out of hand more and more often. Each was as stubborn as the other.

The Night Café, Vincent van Gogh, 1888.

'One evening, after I'd argued with Vincent, I went for a walk to calm down,' Paul later told a friend. 'Suddenly I heard familiar footsteps behind me. I looked over my shoulder and I saw Vincent charging at me with a razor. I must have looked really angry, because he turned around and ran back home. Looking back on it, I've often asked myself whether I should have taken the razor from him and calmed him down. Instead, I went to a hotel. I didn't sleep a wink that night. The next morning, there was a crowd of people standing in front of the yellow house, including some policemen. Vincent had cut off part of his ear. When I walked into Vincent's bedroom, he was rolled up in blankets on his bed. For a moment I thought he was dead. I touched him gingerly, and felt him move. I said to the police: "Wake Vincent gently, and tell him I've gone to Paris."'

When Vincent woke up, he asked for his friend, his pipe and his tobacco. Then he was taken straight to hospital.

That's how Paul's stay in Arles suddenly came to an end after a little over two months. Despite the bad way it ended, it had been an important time for both of them. They had learned a lot from each other. No one could have predicted back then that they would both become world famous.

Vincent van Gogh died on 29 July 1890. Paul would always have warm memories of his friend.

Here are seven details from Paul's 'Café'. Can you find them in the painting? Look on pages 14 and 15.

1

2

3

4

5

The night café – twice

Vincent painted the night café. 'This is one of the ugliest pictures I've ever painted,' he wrote, 'I have tried to express the emotions and sorrows of the people in the café in starkly contrasting reds and greens. I've used as many as seven shades of red and just as many shades of green. The walls are blood red. In the middle of the room there's a vivid green billiard table under the gaslight.' Later, Paul painted the same night café. He didn't paint the whole room, as Vincent had done. Instead, you see Madame Ginoux, the café owner, sitting at a table looking at you. Vincent liked the painting, but Paul wasn't satisfied with it. That's why he later added two figures: the man sitting at the table with the women and the man on the left. The smooth linen canvas painters use for their paintings is expensive, so Paul and Vincent had bought a large roll of coarse jute. It's the same material that's used to make potato sacks. In Arles, Paul painted on this coarse cloth for the first time.

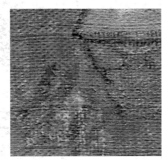
6

Who's in the café to catch mice?

How many sleeping men can you see in both paintings?

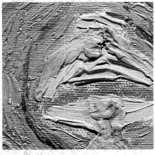
7

What are the thin strings above the billiard table in Paul's night café?

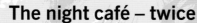

Paul painted with such a thin layer of paint that the canvas shows through. Vincent's thick, smooth strokes of paint have covered the canvas completely. Can you see the difference?

Look on pages 14-15

Do you think there were any other people in Vincent's night café?

Are the people at the back of the café enjoying themselves?

Do the colours red and green harmonise?

19

Get busy!

wall   ceiling

wall

wall

floor

In Vincent's painting, you can almost see the whole café.

wall

floor

Paul only painted part of the café.

Decorate and furnish your own café

WALL
FLOOR

You will need: drawing paper, coloured paper, glue, wax crayons and scissors.

Take two oblong pieces of paper of different colours – one for the floor and the other for the wall. Stick them onto a sheet of drawing paper. What are you going to put in your café? Using wax crayons, colour another sheet of drawing paper completely full with different colours. Then cut out small and large shapes from it to put in your café, such as tables, chairs, glasses or anything else you want. Are there going to be any people in your café? Juggle the shapes around on the sheet, partly overlapping, until you're happy with the way your café looks – then stick them in place.

Large   ...smaller   ...and even smaller
Nearby   ...further away   ...and even further away

Some objects in the painting are partly hidden behind others.

At the edge of the painting you can only see a part of some things.

Different from the rest

In 1889, a world fair was opened in Paris. Countries from all over the world could show their latest innovations in industry, science, trade and art. The Eiffel Tower was built specially for this event. The tower was completely made of steel. For the first time, people could see their entire city, from 300 metres high. Because you could see right through the tower, many people were afraid to go up it.

An art pavilion was also built – le Palais des Beaux-Arts. In this pavilion, a number of French artists were allowed to exhibit their paintings. Paul and his friends weren't invited. So they organised an exhibition in café Volpini in the world fair's grounds. Seventeen of Paul's paintings were on show, together with the work of the others. It was so busy, with the beer-swilling crowd and the bar alongside the wall, that it was hard to get a good look at the paintings. Most people thought the paintings were not very special anyway. But the younger artists particularly liked Paul's work. He was their hero.

People were queuing up to see the pavilion about colonies. Here you could see how people lived in the tropics. There was even an imitation Javanese village, complete with Javanese women who lived there while the exhibition was on. Paul was often to be found in this pavilion. Strolling around among the colourful clothes and exotic objects, he felt like the little boy he had been in Peru.

Along the breezy coast

Paul didn't want to stay in the noisy, overcrowded city of Paris any longer. He set off for peaceful Brittany. But that summer, Pont-Aven was crowded with tourists who had also discovered the village. Paul complained – the village had been ruined by the hordes of people. He went looking for a quiet spot. Twenty kilometres further down the breezy coast he discovered the fishing village of Le Pouldu. Paul and his friends decided to go there.

Bonjour, Monsieur Gauguin, 1889

Haystacks in Brittany, 1890.

In Le Pouldu there was a big house with windows on all sides. Paul and his friend Meijer de Haan were able to rent it cheaply. From the enormous veranda, with a view of the sea, they enjoyed watching the thunder and lightning. The pounding of the waves against the coast shook the house. On the other side the windows overlooked the red sandy plains, the sloping hills and a few farms surrounded by trees. Every day the Breton farmers and farmers' wives walked past the windows with their cows to let them out into the fields. When Paul looked outside he could already see his next painting.

The villagers couldn't get used to the artists. One of the fishermen burst out laughing when Paul walked by. 'What's that oddball doing here, with his long black hair? Why is he trying to dress like a Breton fisherman, with his blue coat and his beret on crooked? The other day I saw him pottering about on the beach – carving arrows out of driftwood. When he tried to shoot them, they just flopped onto the sand. Hasn't he got anything better to do?!'

At the Black Rocks by the Sea, 1889.

Bonjour, Monsieur Gauguin

'Bonjour, Monsieur Gauguin,' the woman in the painting says to Paul. But the gate remains closed. The artist can't get any closer to the woman. When Paul painted this self-portrait he felt lonely and different from everyone else. He didn't feel at home with the people of Le Pouldu, or with the other artists either.

'I don't want to stay here any longer,' Paul thought. 'What would it be like to live in an exotic country again? Would I be happy there? But where could I go?' His dreams of leaving kept haunting him. After much deliberation, he opted for the tropical island of Tahiti.

Look on page 22

The paint in Gauguin's 'Café' is laid on thinly. How is the paint laid on in this painting?

Is it summer in the painting?

What is the fence made of?

Get busy!

1 Two Breton women washing in the river.

The swirling sea

You will need: paper, paint and paintbrushes.

In the watercolour sketche, on page 25, Paul made of the Breton sea the weather was quite calm. Have you ever watched the sea when a storm is raging? Have you watched the high waves with their white crests, pounding against the coast with enormous strength? The water splashes into thousands of tiny droplets. It falls back on itself in a swirling motion, only to rush back in another wave. You can hardly hear yourself speak over the deafening noise. Make a watercolour painting of the sea in this kind of stormy weather. Make the same movements with your paintbrush that the sea makes.

2 Two Breton girls dancing near the haystacks.

What does your landscape look like?

You will need: drawing paper, coloured pencils or paint.

Paul made these three drawings near Le Pouldu. You can only see part of the landscape on them. We have traced the large shapes of Paul's drawings for you. Pick one drawing. Copy the large shapes onto a sheet of paper, imagine what the rest of the landscape looks like, and draw your own Breton landscape. What colours are there in your landscape?

Are there any farms? Do you see hills in the distance, or the sea? Or…

Is the sun shining or are there clouds in the sky? Or…

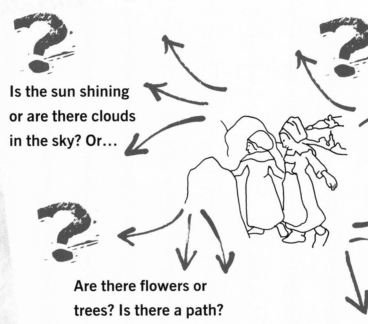

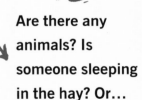

Are there any animals? Is someone sleeping in the hay? Or…

Are there flowers or trees? Is there a path? Or…

3 Breton women beside a fence.

Fatata te Miti

To paradise

Fatata te miti, 1892

In the harbour of Marseilles, on 4 April 1891, the steamboat to Tahiti was ready to depart. Paul went on board. His trunk and his painting equipment were hoisted up on deck, but he held on tight to his small suitcase. The captain called out, 'Cast off!' As the ship sailed out of harbour, the French coast slowly changed into a thin line. The journey would take 63 days. It wasn't the first time that Paul made such a long sea voyage. He took a deep breath to let the fresh sea air flow through his lungs.

On 9 June the ship sailed into the port of Papeete, the capital of Tahiti. Crowds of curious Tahitians were waiting on the quay. They laughed about the strange man walking down the gangplank with his brown felt hat and his long, sun-bleached hair. They were making jokes and calling after him, 'Taata vahine, taata vahine!' At first Paul laughed along with them, but when he discovered that 'Taata vahine' means 'man-woman', he didn't think it was funny any more. He got a haircut. It was much too hot for long hair anyway.

Not what he was searching for

Three days after Paul arrived, Pomare V, the king of Tahiti, died. Thousands of little boats with orange sails sailed out onto the clear blue sea. Everyone hurried to be in time for the funeral. People were pouring into the capital city. The Tahitians were singing special songs to mourn the death of their king. Paul couldn't sleep for the hypnotic music that went on all night. But the next day, life in Papeete went on as if nothing had happened.

After three months in town, Paul was bored to death. The people living there were mostly Europeans, and they were not interested in Tahiti at all. Even worse, they tried to turn the island into a European country. Years earlier, when they had conquered the island, they had made up all kinds of rules. The Tahitians were no longer allowed to sing and dance on the streets. Their art and rituals were forbidden and the women had to wear long dresses. 'No, this isn't what I am searching for,' Paul thought. 'Isn't there anything left of the old Tahiti'? He persuaded Titi, his Tahitian girlfriend, to set off on an adventure with him.

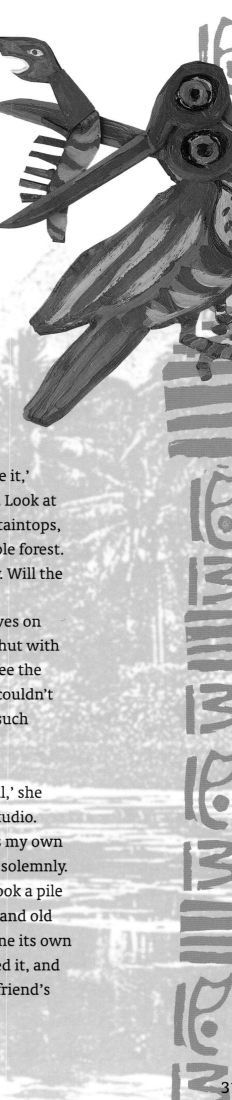

Away from Papeete

When the sun began to rise that morning, Paul and Titi had already
left the town far behind them. With their horse and carriage they rode
on a bumpy, sandy path along the coast. Now and then they passed
a village – a few thatched huts grouped together under palm trees.
Fishermen were already casting their nets into the sea. 'This is more like it,'
Paul said contentedly, 'The light's so bright and the colours are so vivid. Look at
those scarlet flowers! I feel like painting!' He pointed to the bare mountaintops,
rising high above everything else. The hills were covered in impenetrable forest.
'Imagine walking through them on your own. I'd get lost straight away. Will the
dark forest give up its secrets to me?'

    In Mataiea, 45 kilometres from the capital city, they found themselves on
a beautiful, wide beach. When Paul discovered he could rent a bamboo hut with
a palm leaf roof, he was beside himself with joy. On one side, he could see the
mountains. On the other side, he looked out on the glittering sea. Paul couldn't
believe that the sea could be so blue. He would love to be able to paint such
an intense blue.

Meanwhile, Titi had entered the hut. 'It's nice and cool in here, Paul,' she
called. 'Shall we unpack our bags?' Part of the hut became Paul's new studio.
When they had unpacked, the little suitcase was finally opened. 'This is my own
private world of friends – I take them with me wherever I go,' Paul said solemnly.
'That way I can look at them every day, and never be really lonely.' He took a pile
of prints and drawings of his favourite works of art out of the suitcase, and old
photographs of Tahiti, which he had bought in Papeete. He gave each one its own
special place on the wall. Then he picked up a small envelope. He opened it, and
took out some photographs of his children. Titi saw the sadness in her friend's
eyes, and knew how much he missed them.

On the walls of the hut

From his little suitcase, Paul took the pictures he loved. He enjoyed looking at these works of art and photographs. He also used them as subjects in his paintings.

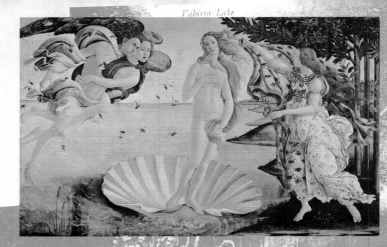

The Birth of Venus, c. 1480, by the Italian painter Sandro Botticelli (1444-1510).

Detail from the Egyptian Book of the Dead, around 3,000 years old.

A mediaeval church window in Canterbury Cathedral, from the 13th century. It's a stained-glass window. Three pilgrims are travelling, with a knapsack, a water jar and a walking stick.

What does your dream island look like?

You will need: 4 sheets of drawing paper, paint, coloured pencils, glue, scissors, photos and pictures you like.

Far, far away, in the middle of the great ocean, is the island of your dreams. It's the place where you would most like to live. You can do anything you like there, and you don't have to do anything you don't want to do. What more could you wish for?

1 Seen from the sky...
You fly to your dream island in a small plane. Before you land you can see what it looks like from the sky. Make a painting of that view.

2 Your first step ashore...
After a smooth landing, you can see everything from close by. Make another painting to show what your desert island looks like. Where will you live?

Adam and Eve (1525), by the German painter Lucas Cranach (1472-1553).

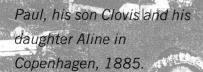

Paul, his son Clovis and his daughter Aline in Copenhagen, 1885.

Picture of a Japanese street by the Japanese artist Utagawa Hiroshige (1797-1858).

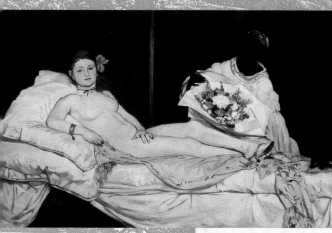

The Olympia, 1863, by the French painter Edouard Manet (1832-1883).

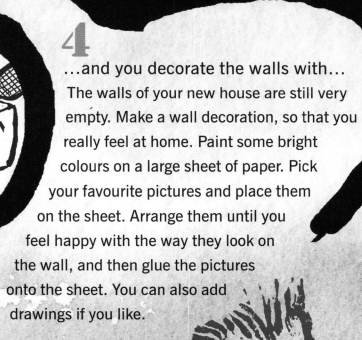

3 I'm going on a journey, so I need…

You can only bring one suitcase to the island. Everything you need has to fit in that suitcase. What can you really not do without? What would really come in handy? Make a painting of the interior of your new house. Decorate it with the things you took with you.

4 …and you decorate the walls with…

The walls of your new house are still very empty. Make a wall decoration, so that you really feel at home. Paint some bright colours on a large sheet of paper. Pick your favourite pictures and place them on the sheet. Arrange them until you feel happy with the way they look on the wall, and then glue the pictures onto the sheet. You can also add drawings if you like.

Get busy!

Vahine no te tiare, 1891. A Tahitian woman wears a fresh flower in her hair every day.

Haere mai venez!, 1891. (Come here!) Pigs foraging in the Tahitian landscape.

Street in Tahiti, 1891. Near Papeete.

Can he read my thoughts?

Paul started to explore his surroundings, looking for things to paint. He had unpacked his empty canvases and laid out his paints. He couldn't wait to get started. After a few weeks, Titi started to complain. 'It's so quiet out here, and there is nothing for me to do.' One day she packed her things and left for Papeete.

That night Paul was lying alone in his hut for the first time. He hardly dared to turn over – the tropical night was so quiet. All he could hear was the rustle of leaves, the whisper of the palm trees and the lonely cry of a bird in the distance. The moonlight shone through the cracks in the walls of the hut. Paul felt sad and lonely. For weeks he hadn't received any post from his friends in Paris. Not even his wife Mette had sent him a letter. Had they forgotten him already? And where was the money he still had to receive from the sale of his paintings? He only had enough food for two more days.

The following morning, his neighbour came to see him. Using sign language, he invited him over for breakfast. 'Can he read my thoughts?' Paul wondered. He timidly shook his head. A few moments later, a little girl came to his hut. She placed some food, wrapped up in fresh leaves, on the doorstep, then walked away without saying a word. From that moment on, the ice was broken and Paul had a chat with his neighbour every day.

The Meal, 1891. With three Tahitian children.

Upa Upa, 1891. A fire dance in Tahiti.

Nearby lived a beautiful Tahitian lady. Paul invited her to his hut. When she realised that Paul wanted to paint her picture, she suddenly disappeared. 'Why does she have to walk away?' Paul thought, irritated. 'Just when I thought I'd found myself a beautiful model…' Then, just as quickly as she had left, the lady reappeared. She had changed into her loveliest long dress, and put a fresh flower in her hair, especially for him. He would rather have painted her in her pareu – the colourful, floral cloth that Tahitians wear loosely around their hips. The painting he made of her, 'Vahine no te tiare', was his first portrait of a Tahitian lady.

Looking for company

Without Titi for company, it was much too quiet in Paul's hut. He couldn't get on with his painting. 'I'm going to look for a new girlfriend,' Paul thought, and he decided to tour the island looking for one.

On his way, Paul passed through the village of Faone. A man greeted him: 'Aloha! Where are you going? Aren't you the painter? Come and eat with us.' Paul didn't need to be asked twice, and he got off his horse. Together they went into a hut. A man and a woman were chatting and laughing inside.

The woman asked, 'What are you looking for?' 'I'm looking for a girlfriend,' Paul answered. 'There are a lot of beautiful women in Faone,' she said. She pointed at a young woman who had just entered with the food. 'What do you think of my daughter Tehura?' Paul greeted the beautiful girl. She sat down on the ground next to him. She delicately placed some food on a large banana leaf. 'Will you make her happy?' her mother asked. 'Then she can come with you.'

Man with an Axe, 1891.

Nafea Faa ipoipoi, 1892. 'When will you marry?' one woman asks another.

Together with Tehura

'This is one of the happiest times of my life,' Paul would later write about his time with Tehura. He was trying more and more to live like a real Tahitian. But when one day Paul tried on a pareu, Tehura doubled up with laughter: 'A cloth around your hips like that – it just doesn't suit you.'

Paul adored the scenery, the beautiful women, and the colours. There was more than enough to paint. But still something was gnawing at him. He had imagined life on the island completely differently. He had thought he could live off the land, and that it would be quiet and peaceful. Still, he knew for sure that the paradise of his dreams had once existed in Tahiti. So he started looking for everything he could find about the old Tahiti and he dreamed of that world, where he wanted so much to live himself. In his paintings, he brought this world to life in bright colours and bold shapes. He painted for hours on end like a man possessed. Artists' materials were lying around all over his hut, and everything smelled of wet oil paint. Lots of new paintings were stacked up against the walls.

...raro te oviri, 1891. People are working under the tropical palm trees on the beach.

Arearea, 1892. A woman playing a flute, with a red dog.

In the dark hut

Tehura never complained about Paul painting all the time. Sometimes, she would sit motionless on the floor for hours on end. At times like this, if Paul asked her, 'Tehura, what are you thinking about?' she never answered, as if she was very far away in another world that he knew nothing of. Paul longed to join her there. He tried to get her to tell him the stories of Tahiti she had heard from her grandmother. When she started talking about the spirits of her ancestors, shivers ran down her spine. But it didn't occur to Paul that Tehura believed in the mysterious stories so deeply, until…

One day he had to go to Papeete to get the post and to buy oil for the lamp. He promised to return that same evening. On the way back the carriage stopped halfway, and Paul had to walk the rest of the way. He didn't get back until one in the morning. When he opened the door, he saw that the light had gone out. For a moment he thought that Tehura had run away. Quickly, Paul struck a match. Tehura was lying on the bed, stock-still. She looked at him with wide, frightened eyes, but she didn't recognise him. Paul was shocked, but at the same time he thought how enchantingly beautiful she was. In order not to frighten Tehura even more, he didn't dare to move. When she finally realised that it was Paul, she cried out, 'Don't ever leave me alone again in the dark! I thought you were a tupapau, an angry spirit of my ancestors.' Paul took her in his arms and tried to comfort her. This experience made such an impression on him that he made the painting 'Manao Tupapau'.

Manao Tupapau, 1892.

Can you find the ghost in the painting? What does it look like?

Can you see where Paul has used contrasting colours in the painting Manao Tupapau? You can read about contrasting colours on pages 12 and 13.

There are no lights on, yet it's not completely dark in the hut. Can you see where the light in the painting is coming from?

Homesick

Paul was standing on the quay of the harbour in Papeete. A plume of smoke from the mail boat appeared on the horizon. 'I hope my money is finally in the post,' Paul thought. 'How else am I going to pay for my journey home? I've never been able to work so well as I have in the past year. And yet, I still want to go home. I feel ill and exhausted and I'm homesick for my family and friends. When shall I tell Tehura that I'm going back to France? The thought of leaving her here makes me feel sad already.'

In this chapter you see several paintings by Paul which he made in Tahiti. Which painting do you think is the most

mysterious? --

exotic? ---

dreamy? --

cheerful? ---

scary? --

like a paradise? ---

Golden death mask of the Egyptian pharaoh Tutankhamen, around 3340 years old.

Statues on Easter Island, 9 metres high and around 3000 years old.

Parahi Te Marae, There lies the temple, 1892.

The sacred hill in the painting is shining bright yellow in the sunlight. A great statue towers above the mountain. It's the moon goddess Hina. She's sitting in front of the entrance to a temple. A plume of smoke is curling up from the holy fire. Sacrifices are being made to the gods. No one is allowed to go near the temple. That's why there's a fence around it. But in fact there were no temples or statues of gods on Tahiti. Paul took his ideas from all over the world. His collection of photographs came in handy for this. He used a moon goddess from Easter Island, a Buddha from Asia and pictures of the pharaohs from Egypt to create his own 'Hina'. In his paintings, he set all these figures against the background of the Tahitian landscape.

Sitting Buddha from Thailand.

Get busy!

If you draw with a coloured pencil, you can add some water and smudge it out a little with your finger.

Painting on canvas with a firm brush.

Draw carefully with your pencil or crayon on coarse-textured paper or card.

Dreams on paper or canvas

You will need: drawing paper, watercolours, paint in a tube, paintbrushes, coloured pencils and wax crayon.

In your dreams you can do wonderful things. You can fly, or do all sorts of things. When you wake up it's suddenly over and you're lying in your bed. Do you remember one of those dreams you would like to get back into? Make a drawing or painting of that dream. To show that it's a dream you can use vague shapes and soft colours. To do this you can choose one of the drawing and painting techniques described on these pages. You can also combine some of them.

Use your paint straight from the tube on coarse paper. Don't use water.

zzzzz

If you first moisten your paper a little with a sponge and then paint using watercolours, you'll see that the paint runs.

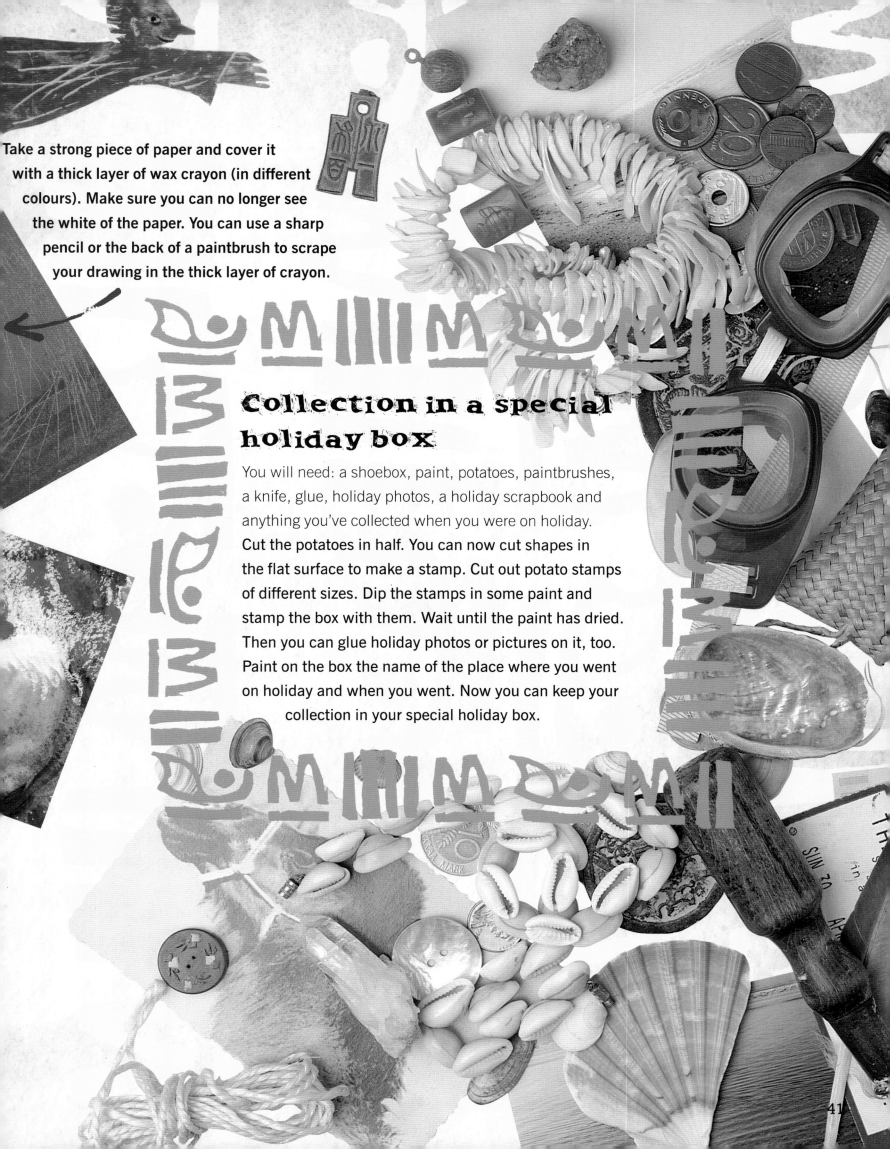

Take a strong piece of paper and cover it with a thick layer of wax crayon (in different colours). Make sure you can no longer see the white of the paper. You can use a sharp pencil or the back of a paintbrush to scrape your drawing in the thick layer of crayon.

Collection in a special holiday box

You will need: a shoebox, paint, potatoes, paintbrushes, a knife, glue, holiday photos, a holiday scrapbook and anything you've collected when you were on holiday. Cut the potatoes in half. You can now cut shapes in the flat surface to make a stamp. Cut out potato stamps of different sizes. Dip the stamps in some paint and stamp the box with them. Wait until the paint has dried. Then you can glue holiday photos or pictures on it, too. Paint on the box the name of the place where you went on holiday and when you went. Now you can keep your collection in your special holiday box.

Noa Noa

Paul arrived in Marseilles on 30 August 1893 without a penny in his pocket. Tired from the long journey, he wanted to get to Paris as quickly as possible. To his great surprise there was an envelope with money in it waiting for him at the post office. His friend Daniel de Monfreid had taken care of that. Now he could take the next train.

When he arrived in Paris he discovered that his friends were in Pont-Aven. So Paul had to be patient a little longer before he could show them his work. Unexpectedly, he inherited some money from his uncle Zizi in Orleans. This came in very handy; Paul rented a fine, spacious studio on the rue Vercingétorix.

Visiting Paul

On a bleak autumn day Paul impatiently opened the gate and looked out into the street to see if the poet Charles Morice was coming yet. When his friend turned the corner he raised his hand. 'Good to see you Paul. How are you? I hardly recognise you!' Paul looked like an oriental prince. His face was tanned by the tropical sun. He was wearing a velvet beret on his head and his coat was hanging loosely around his shoulders, like a cape. Together they walked through the courtyard, past the big old tree, and up the stairs to the first floor of the building. 'I've found a wonderful studio,' Paul said. 'Come on, I'll show you.' He opened the front door and showed Charles into the small front room. In the corner there was a big bed covered with a floral pareu. Colourful rugs were scattered on the floor. A parrot kept on screeching until Paul threw a cloth over the cage. Paul motioned for Charles to follow him. Through a glass door they entered a large studio. Paul had painted the windows yellow. It made the light warm, as if the sun was shining every day.

'Just step over those rolls,' Paul said. 'I had to take my paintings off their wooden canvas stretchers and roll them up. Otherwise I couldn't have taken everything with me on the ship. I've made more than eighty paintings. My portfolio is bulging with drawings. And I couldn't even bring all of my wooden statues.'

'And did you bring those beautiful weapons from Tahiti as well?' Charles asked. Paul shook his head and laughed. 'I bought those in Paris. You can't find them in Tahiti anymore.'

'I've already framed a few of the paintings, but I still have to stretch most of them. I'm curious to hear what you think of them. You're the first of my friends to see them.' Charles' face lit up as Paul unrolled one painting after another for him. 'Incredible, Paul! I hadn't expected this. I can hardly believe you were really there. What beautiful paintings! The others have really got to see these. Gosh, you've been working so hard.'

There were words in the paintings in a language Charles didn't understand. 'What do those words mean, Paul? It looks like some kind of secret language.' Then Paul started telling him all about Tahiti and the people he met there, and, of course, about Tehura. Hours later they said goodbye. Charles said, 'It would be a pity if you didn't do something with those stories. Maybe you can write a book about them. I'd like to help you with that.'

The news that Paul was back spread quickly. More and more people found their way to his studio. Meanwhile the olive green and yellow walls were filled with his new paintings. On Thursday evenings in particular, lots of young writers and poets would visit Paul. They talked and laughed a lot. But as soon as Paul started reading from his journal, everybody fell silent. The stories about the unknown paradise captivated them all.

Paul's friends were also very enthusiastic about his new paintings. But the strange subjects and titles in Tahitian scared people off a bit. That's why Paul decided it would be a good idea to write a book. It would be called 'Noa Noa', the Tahitian word for 'fragrant'. When people read that they would surely understand his work better.

Some pages from Paul's notebook for Noa Noa.

How many dogs are there in the woodcut?

Carving a drawing in wood is not as simple as drawing on paper. Can you see that the lines in the wood are different?

TRICK QUESTION: Just like with a potato stamp, you cut away what you don't want to use. For every new colour you use another woodblock. How many blocks did Paul use? Remember what you have read about mixing paint.

Woodcuts for Noa Noa, 1893-1894

I see a tree with a dream. Can you find it too? What do you see in the dream?

What are the women wearing?

Woodcuts for the book Noa Noa

Noa Noa is about Tehura, about the Tahitian gods and living closely with nature. Some of the stories are true; others were made up by Paul. But when you read them, it's just as if they really happened. On Tahiti, Paul used a notebook. It's full of watercolour drawings, sketches and photos. He could use these notes and pictures for his book Noa Noa. Paul made ten woodcuts for the book. He tried all sorts of things. Sometimes he used white paper, and other times he used coloured paper. That's why every print is slightly different.

A print for Charles

Paul held up a wooden board for Charles to see. 'I'm making a woodcut for Noa Noa,' he said. He had cut out a drawing in the wood. 'I'm going to print this one for you.' He first put some ink on the board and placed a sheet of paper on it. When he then put the board on his bed and lay on top of it, Charles called out, 'What are you doing?' 'Making a print, I told you!' Paul answered, and laughed. He carefully pulled the paper from the board and looked at the print closely. He put his name on it and gave it to Charles. 'This is for you. But don't forget to let the ink dry!'

A solo exhibition

Paul was offered a solo exhibition at Durand-Ruel, the best-known modern art gallery in Paris. Now he really belonged! Great artists, such as Claude Monet, Edgar Degas, Camille Pissarro and Auguste Renoir, had all exhibited their work there. Important collectors often came there to buy paintings.

When the doors of the gallery opened in November 1894, people flooded in. It isn't hard to imagine what it was like to step out of the cold winter into Paul's warm tropical world. Everyone gazed, fascinated, at the 44 huge paintings, their bright colours reflecting on the walls. All the art lovers were talking about it. Some were enthusiastic; but others thought the paintings were strange and didn't like the colours.

The hut on the beach, the beautiful woman at Paul's side and life amidst unspoiled nature – everyone loved it. Still, only eleven paintings in the gallery were sold.

No matter how much Paul loved being back among his friends, he couldn't get used to the city, with its chilly streets and its dreary buildings anymore. What was he supposed to paint, without nature and beautiful women around him? He wished he was back in Tahiti with the people he felt so at home with. At least he could work in peace there. He made plans to return to the island. On 3 July he departed for Tahiti for the second time.

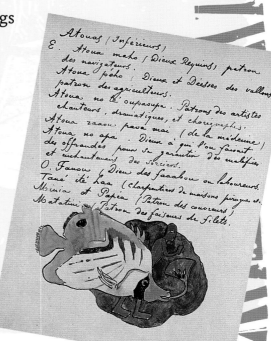

Is your hair curly or straight?

Are your eyes big or small?

Is your head round or oval?

Do your ears stick out, or are they very small?

And what's the shape of your mouth?

Is your nose pointed or turned up?

Hello, this is me

You will need: a large sheet of paper, felt-tip pens, coloured paper, magazines, photos, colouring pencils, paint and brushes, scissors and glue. Look in the mirror carefully. Make a simple drawing of your face with a black pencil. Glue pieces of coloured paper onto your drawing. You can find coloured paper everywhere – in magazines, wrapping paper, floral wallpaper, squared paper, and so on.

and I love...

Fill in the gaps:

My favourite animal is --

My favourite colour is --

My hobbies are --

My favourite food is --

My favourite pop star is --

I like going to --

And --

You can stick all kinds of things that you like around your self-portrait. Find pictures or photos of all your favourite things. You can also draw or paint them. Put everything on your self-portrait and arrange it until you have made a good picture. Then stick everything down. That's how you make your own collage.

You can also
add a map
of your house,
garden, bedroom
or the street where
you live.

No te aha oe riri, 1896

49

A Tahitian family are sitting in front of their hut. The women are wearing pareus with flowers.

TAHITI 1895

Even though there was electric light in Papeete now, and music was blaring from a gramophone in the main street, Paul was sure of one thing: he never wanted to go back to France. He rented a plot of land in Puna'auia, 32 kilometres from the capital. It was near the road, and nice and cool in the shade of some large trees. With the help of his neighbours he built a large hut. Strange statues stood jumbled together in the tall grass around the hut. The statue of a lioness playing with her cub attracted a lot of attention. 'Do such big cats really exist?' asked the people from the village. They were also amazed by the French sunflowers, irises and gladioli that Paul had planted in his garden.

In the new studio, which was twenty metres long by eight metres wide, not a piece had remained undecorated. Paul had carved all kinds of figures in the wooden beams. On the walls were colourful cloths, illustrations, and, of course, his photos. The old Persian rug he took with him wherever he went lay on the floor.

Disaster after disaster

In 1897 Paul suddenly had to move his hut. The owner of the land had died and he couldn't rent the place any longer. That was not the only disaster. His money didn't get sent to him. And he was often too ill to work. He had also given up hope that one day he would see his wife and children again. He had made a special book for his daughter Aline. In it, he had written everything he wanted to tell her, complete with little drawings. The last time he had seen Aline was seven years before. She was thirteen years old then. It was time to send her the book, so that

Paul's hut in Puna'auia. The painting 'Where Do We Come From? What Are We? Where Are We Going?' is standing outside to dry.

she could still get to know him a little. Then, unexpectedly, Paul received a letter from Mette. Aline had died of pneumonia. Nothing could comfort him now. Paul didn't want to go on living.

His last wish was to make one special painting. It was to be his masterpiece, his very best work. It would be very big, so he would need lots of paint and paintbrushes. He worked on it non-stop, without resting, and hardly even taking time to eat. He wanted to put all his feelings into this painting.

After a month it was finished. Paul was completely exhausted. He bought a bottle of arsenic – a very powerful poison. In the evening, he walked up into the mountains, intending to kill himself. Paul probably took too much of the poison. It made him vomit, so it didn't work. Dangerously ill, he dragged himself back to his hut. For a week he could only stare at the painting from his bed.

Paul wrote about the painting: 'I've painted directly onto the canvas, without making a sketch first. The canvas is coarse and uneven. You will probably say it is sloppily painted and not nearly finished. But for me it is finished. And I believe that I will never again paint a better picture.'

In the painting, Paul shows the different phases of life. You are born, you grow up, you become older and eventually you die. People of different ages are sitting together on a riverbank. On the right, a baby lies asleep. He has his whole life ahead of him. The boy in the middle is curious. He is wondering, 'Where did I come from? What am I? And where am I going? What will my future look like?' To get the answers to his questions he picks a fruit from the Tree of Knowledge. The old woman, on the left of the painting, doesn't need this fruit anymore. She's looking back on the life she has had.

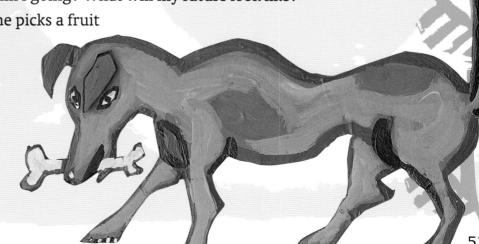

Where Do We Come From? What Are We? Where Are We Going?, 1897.

I spy… two red dots in the distance…
What are they?

What is the girl in
the foreground eating?
Who could she have
got it from?

Paul wants to give us the
impression that the painting
is painted on an old, yellow
wall. That's why he painted
the upper corners yellow.
Can you see what's written
in those yellow corners?

How many
people are there
in the painting?

Paul often painted animals in
his paintings. What animals can
you see in this painting?

Not his last painting after all

Paul was not to paint many pictures in the next five years. In March 1898 he had to find a job in Papeete to pay his debts. After five months, he returned to Puna'auia. His hut was in ruins. Rats had gnawed holes in the roof. The rain had destroyed the things that were still in the hut, and cockroaches had spoiled a large pile of drawings.

Paul was very surprised when he suddenly received a letter from Ambroise Vollard, an art dealer from Paris. Vollard was interested in Paul's paintings. The art dealer thought they could turn out to be worth a lot of money. In exchange for 24 paintings a year Paul would receive a small monthly allowance. At last he had no more money worries. He wanted to celebrate that. He ordered some special delicacies and fine French wine to treat his neighbours to a feast.

How can you decode this message?

.gnitniap eht ot
dnatsrednu t'nac uoy
eht no srettel egral
eht detniap luaP
eht daer nac uoy sngis
eht ot txen llaw eht
ereht muesum a nI

Make up your own secret language

You will need: drawing paper, pencils and paint.
The words on Paul's Tahitian paintings seem to be in
a secret language. They sound very mysterious. Have
you ever made your own secret language? Think of
a story or something exciting you have seen. Write it
in a secret language on a sheet of drawing paper.
You can illustrate it with a drawing or collage. Is there
anyone who can decode your language?

busy!

gnoleb od yeht ,meht

hguoht nevE .savnac

htiw naitihaT ni seltit

.gnitniap eht fo eltit

esoht nO .sgnitniap

no sngis llams era

Conch Shell

They have brought me a conch shell.

Within it sings
a map sized sea.
My heart
fills up with water
and little fish
of shadow and silver.

They have brought me a conch shell.

This is a poem by the Spanish poet
Federico García Lorca (1898-1936).

Paint a poem

You will need: coarse paper or canvas,
paintbrushes and paint.
Paul loved poems. Poems leave a lot to your
imagination. If you read the poem 'Conch Shell,'
what do you see before you? Make a painting
of what you see. You could also choose your
own poem. Use a coarse background for the
painting, just like Paul did. That will make it less
focused. Then everyone can look at your painting
and imagine things. On page 40 you will find
some examples of painting techniques. Paint
the title of your poem on it.

Even further away

Riders on the Beach, 1902

For years, Paul had had the idea to go to the Marquesas Islands, a group of tiny islands in the middle of the Pacific Ocean. In the Papeete museum he had seen objects that were made by the Maoris, the inhabitants of the Marquesas. No matter whether they are oars or fruit bowls, the extraordinary woodcarving makes them true works of art.

Now that he no longer needed to worry about money, Paul decided to go to Hiva Oa, the largest of the Marquesas Islands. He sold his hut, packed his bags and left.

How Paul got a plot of land

In September 1901 Paul arrived in the capital, Atuona. He wanted to buy a plot of land. To his great surprise, all the land belonged to the church. The Maoris didn't have much power on their own island. How would he be able to get a plot of land now? For three weeks, Paul went to church, just to make a good impression. The bishop was tricked by Paul's hypocrisy and Paul was allowed to buy a piece of land. When he didn't come to church afterwards, the bishop felt really foolish!

Paul's new hut was in the middle of the village. Because the overgrowth was so dense, you couldn't see the hut from the road.

In the mornings, Paul would sit in the sun on his veranda. A cool ocean breeze stopped it from getting too hot. It was nice and quiet, and it didn't cost much money. With a shop nearby where he could buy anything he needed, he was as happy as could be.

A wooden oar from Easter Island. The woodcarving resembles that of the Maoris on the Marquesas Islands.

A crown made on the Marquesas Islands from pieces of tortoiseshell and shells.

His neighbour Tioka often visited him. They would talk about the island. Or they went to the beach – the meeting place of the Maoris, where people told each other the latest gossip and news, but also old Maori stories. In no time, they saw Paul as one of them. 'Koki, Koki,' they would call when he passed by. The Europeans looked annoyed when they heard Paul's Maori name. They couldn't understand how this strange artist got along so well with the Maoris.

Mmm... human flesh

There was often an old man sitting on the beach. They said he had been in prison for cannibalism – eating human flesh. One day he said, 'I've lived through the time when we Maori warriors went to war with each other. When an enemy died, we ate him.'

'And…,' Paul asked, 'does human flesh taste good?' The eyes in the wrinkled face started to twinkle. 'We only ate Maori flesh, because European flesh is not so tasty. You belong with us. If I look at you, my mouth starts to water. But I don't have a quarrel with you, so I won't eat you. I will protect your house against evil spirits with a good spell.'

Paul stands up for the Maoris

Just as in Tahiti, the Europeans had set strict rules for the Maoris. The police constantly kept a close eye on them. They were fined for any breach of the rules. Paul tried to help the Maoris solve their problems. The governors warned Paul not to interfere. But Paul didn't bother about these warnings. On 31 March 1903 he was even sentenced to three months in prison and a heavy fine.

Tiki, a stone ancestor figure from the Marquesas Islands.

Painting becomes more difficult

One of the last large paintings that Paul made in Hiva Oa is that of the riders on the beach. The colours are much lighter than in the paintings he had made in Tahiti. If only he was well enough, then he could finally finish the painting that was in his studio. But he couldn't even manage to hold a paintbrush. The only thing he could still do was to make a small drawing every now and then, or to write something. The agreement with Vollard to send 24 paintings a year became a heavy burden.

Desperately, Paul wrote to his friend Daniel: 'Actually, I don't want to leave this place, but I often feel so unwell that I can't even stand up. And I can't see very well any more. I need a good doctor, but there aren't any here. That's why I want to return to France.'

'You'd better not come back,' his friend replied. 'That wouldn't be good for the sales of your work. Now you're the artist who lives far away in an unknown paradise. People find that interesting. They're beginning to like your work more and more.'

A wooden statue Paul made of the goddess Hina and the god Te Fatu, 1892

Can you find these animals in the book? Complete the page numbers:

 page…

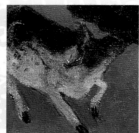 page…

 page…

 page…

 page…

 page…

 page…

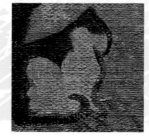 page…

 page…

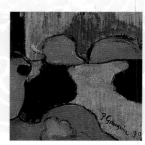 page…

Get busy!

Cut out the nose, but leave the top fixed.

Twined cord with beads. You can stick feathers in it.

Elastic bands to tighten the mask behind your ears.

Paint patterns with lines of paint.

Mask in the jungle

You will need: thick cardboard (e.g., from an old box), paint, a cord, elastic band, scissors, a paintbrush, strong glue and things to decorate your mask with, such as beads, sunflower seeds, feathers, shells, buttons…
Cut the shape of your mask from the cardboard. Keep in mind where your eyes and mouth should go. Paint it and decorate it with everyday things.

Unravelled cord.

'Na mate Koki! Na pete enate!'

Paul woke up very early that morning. He hadn't slept well because of the terrible pain he felt. He waited for Tioka, who came to visit him every morning to see if he was all right. When he heard footsteps in the garden, he called out desperately, 'Tioka, I feel terrible! Please ask Paul Vernier to come and see me.' Tioka was shocked when he saw how pale Paul's face was. He hurried to get Paul Vernier, the vicar. When he got to the school, a kilometre away, he ran into the classroom. The vicar was in the middle of a French lesson with a class of children. 'You have to come with me right now! Paul Gauguin isn't well!'

They reached the hut, breathless. The preacher pulled a chair next to the bed and sat down with Paul. Paul complained that he was hurting all over, but after a while he changed the subject. He talked about a beautiful book he was reading. By talking to his friend, Paul forgot the pain for a while. After an hour he said, 'You don't have to worry. I feel much better now that I've talked to you. Isn't it time to return to your pupils?'

Around eleven o'clock Paul's cook came tearing into the classroom. 'Come quickly! The white man is dead!' For the second time that morning, Paul Vernier went to the hut. He found Tioka by the bed, completely distraught. 'I came by to see how he was doing. I called from the garden, "Koki, Koki." But he didn't answer. Then I ran quickly upstairs. Koki was lying still on his bed. He was dead.' After Tioka had said this, he bit Paul Gauguin hard in the head. He was trying to bring him back to life again. But it didn't work. 'Na mate Koki. Na pete enate!' Tioka called. 'Paul Gauguin is dead. We are lost!'

Father of modern art

In one of Paul's last letters to Daniel de Monfreid he wrote: 'You know what I have wanted to achieve as an artist. I wanted to dare everything, without bothering about what others would think about it. I didn't quite manage that. It's not my paintings, but my ideas that count. The painters of today will profit from the freedom for which I have fought so hard.'

And Paul was right. In the great exhibition of 1906, young artists such as Henri Matisse, Raoul Duffy and Pablo Picasso discovered his paintings. Paul became a hero to them, an example to follow. Paul Gauguin is one of the fathers of modern art in the twentieth century. After him, everything was possible.

Illustrations

All paintings are Gauguin's, unless otherwise stated.

We have made every effort to contact the copyright holders of the source material used in this book. We apologize to anyone we have been unable to reach and welcome information which will allow us to improve or correct our copyright acknowledgements in any subsequent reprinting.

Bibliography

• Becker, Christoph et al., Paul Gauguin: Tahiti, Stuttgart, 1998
• Bern, Maurice, Victor Segalen. Voyager et Visionair, Paris, 1999
• Boyle-Turner, Caroline, Gauguin and the School of Pont-Aven, London, 1986
• Denvir, Bernard, The Search for Paradise: Gauguin's Letters from Brittany and the South Seas, London, 1992
• Gauguin, Paul, Noa Noa, San Francisco, 1994
• Gauguin, Paul, Gauguin's Letters from the South Seas, London, 1992
• Gauguin, Paul, Gauguin's Intimate Journals, London, 1996
• Goldwater, Robert, Paul Gauguin: Das Verlorene Paradies, Cologne, 1998 (Catalogue)
• Federico García Lorca, 'Conch Shell'
• Nemeczek, Alfred, Van Gogh in Arles, Munich, 1999
• Newton, Douglas, Arts of the South Seas, Munich, London, New York, 1999
• Stevenson, Lesley, Gauguin, London, 1995
• Thomson, Belinda, Gauguin, Cambridge, 1990
• Thomson, Belinda, Gauguin by Himself, Cambridge, 1998

Colophon

Concept, text, illustrations, graphic design: Ceciel de Bie and Martijn Leenen, Amsterdam
Cover illustration: Majel, Amsterdam
Consultant: Sjraar van Heugten
Translation: Baxter Associates, Hilversum
Lithography: Snoeck-Ducaju & Zoon, Gent
Printer: Snoeck-Ducaju & Zoon, Gent
Publisher: V+K Publishing, Blaricum

Answers

Page 10

The river is at the top of the painting.

Paul has used the colours red, white, black, yellow, green, brown, blue and grey

No, you can't see the individual blades.

You can't see the faces of the women clearly.

Page 19

There are four sleeping men in the two paintings.

The cat's in the café to catch mice.

Many people are smoking in the painting, because you can see wisps of smoke.

The people do not seem to be enjoying themselves.

Yes, there were more people in the café, because there are empty glasses and bottles on the tables.

No, the colours green and red contrast.

Page 25

Some parts are painted in thick layers of paint, for example, the coat and the bushes; other parts are painted in thin layers of paint, for example, the sky and the grass.

It's winter, because there are no leaves on the trees.

The fence is made of thick branches.

Page 44

There are two little dogs in the woodcut.

The lines are less flowing than on a normal drawing.

The tree looks like a dream cloud with people and trees in it.

The women wear a pareu and a blouse.

Paul used three woodblocks, one for black, one for yellow and one for red. The orange is made by printing yellow and red on top of each other.

Page 52

The two red dots in the distance are the roofs of houses.

The girl in the foreground is eating a piece of fruit from the tree. She probably got it from the boy.

There are 12 people in the painting.

The animals in the painting are a cat, a goat, a dog, a white bird, a coloured bird, a lizard and, in the upper corner, a deer.

In the left upper corner Paul has written, 'D'ou venons nous? Que sommes nous? Ou allons nous?' That's the title of the painting in French. In the right upper corner you can see Paul's signature.

Page 60

You can find the details on:

page 49   page 6   page 8   page 37   page 11

    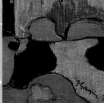

page 22   page 52   page 14   page 26   page 24

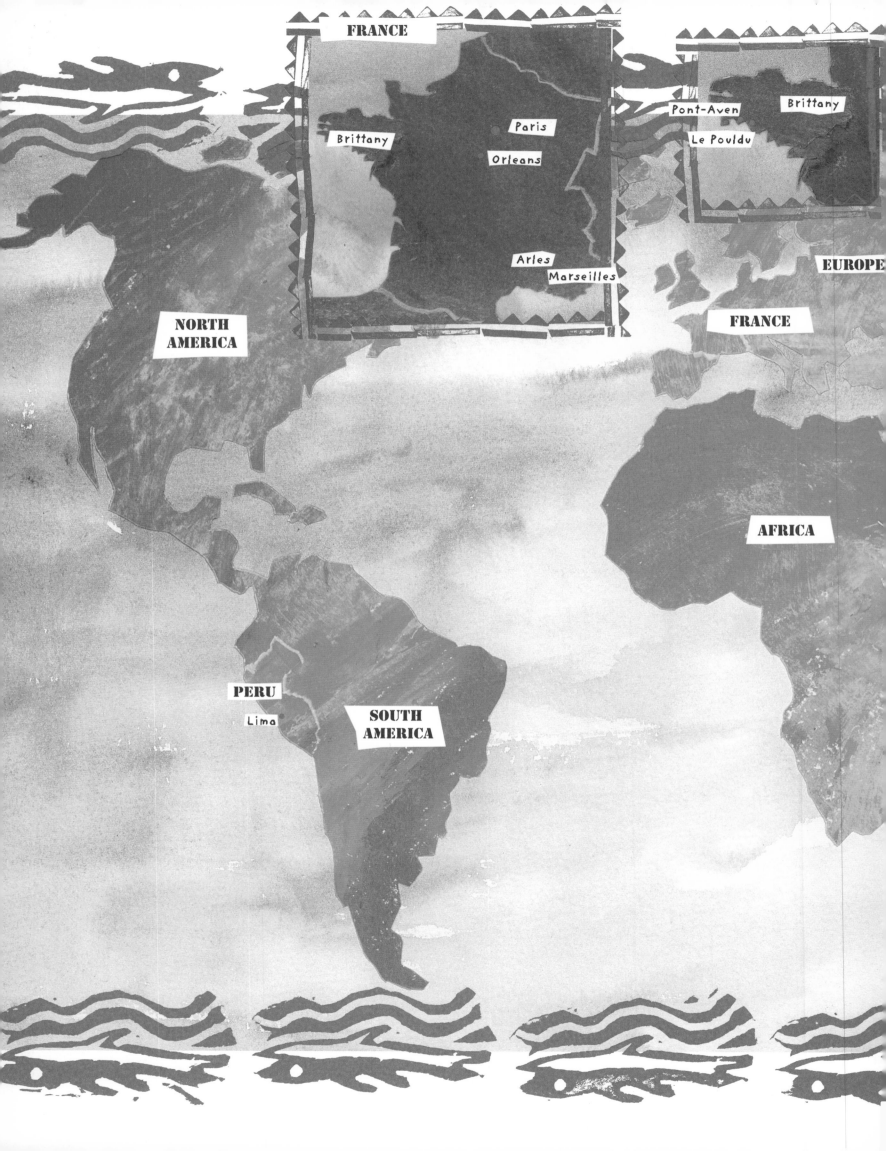

FRANCE

Brittany

Paris

Orleans

Arles

Marseilles

Pont-Aven

Le Pouldu

Brittany

EUROPE

FRANCE

NORTH
AMERICA

AFRICA

PERU

Lima

SOUTH
AMERICA